SO-CWT-195

How to Talk to Your Mate

H. NORMAN WRIGHT

POCKET GUIDES
Tyndale House Publishers, Inc.
Wheaton, Illinois

Adapted from *Communication: Key to Your Marriage* by H. Norman
Wright, copyright 1974 by Regal Books. Used by permission.

Unless otherwise noted, Scripture quotations are from *The Living Bible*,
copyright 1971 held by assignment to Illinois Regional Bank N.A. (as
trustee). All rights reserved.

Library of Congress Catalog Card Number 89-50078
ISBN 0-8423-1378-8
Copyright 1989 by Tyndale House Publishers
All rights reserved
Printed in the United States of America

3   4   5   6   7   8   92

CONTENTS

The Future of Marriage

Does the institution called "marriage" have a future?

Some experts are saying that marriage as we now know it is on the way out. As divorce rates continue to climb—or at least stay at appallingly high levels—many people are growing pessimistic about marriage. Even for seemingly "perfectly matched" couples, marriage grows to be more and more of a gamble.

Three major changes are taking place in the institution of marriage today:

1. A decline in understanding between marriage partners

2. The loss of determination to stay married

3. The development of unrealistic marriage expectations

Decline of understanding and lack of communication go together. Many couples today lack the kind of communication skills that produce the understanding necessary for a marriage to grow strong or even exist.

Understanding in a marriage doesn't mean there are no differences. It does mean that you and your mate are able to talk about the differences and come to an understanding of each other's views. You are able to accept the fact that your partner was raised in a different fashion and because of that will react differently than you. Just because something was done in a certain manner in your home when you were growing up does not mean it has to be done that same way in your new home.

Two people who love one another but are unable to understand each other suffer pain—a continual biting pain—in their relationship. Understanding may not come easily, but a willingness to share views, to see the "other side of the question," to talk things out, can help a husband and wife adjust and adapt to their honest differences of opinion.

Someone has likened this adjustment to two porcupines who lived in Alaska. When the deep and heavy snows came they felt the cold and began to draw close together. However, when they drew close they began to stick one another with their quills. When they drew apart they felt the cold once again. In order to keep warm they had to learn how to adjust to one another.

Lack of determination to stay married is seen frequently today. To have had more than one husband or wife is not considered at all unusual. As one woman filled out an application for a new job, she came to the question, "Married or Single?" Her answer: "Between marriages."

Many enter marriage today with the attitude that if they do not get along they can break the relationship and try again. Many people are too impatient with their marriages. They do not want to live "happily ever after." They want to live "happily right away," and when this does not happen, they bail out.

Too many young couples enter marriage blinded by unrealistic expectations. They believe the relationship should be characterized by a high level of continuous romantic love. As one young adult said: "I wanted marriage to fulfill all my desires. I needed security, someone to take care of me, intellectual stimulation, and economic security immediately—but it just wasn't like that!" People are looking for something "magical" to happen in marriage.

But magic doesn't make a marriage work; hard work does. When there are positive results it is because of two people working together one step at a time.

Charles Shedd, in his book *Letters to Phillip,* tells the story of two rivers flowing smoothly and quietly along until they came together and joined. When this happened they clashed and hurled themselves at one another. As the newly formed river flowed downstream, however, it gradually quieted down and flowed smoothly again. But now it was much broader, more majestic, and had much more power.

Dr. Shedd suggests that "A good marriage is often like that. When two independent streams of existence come together, there will probably be some dashing of life against life at the juncture. Personalities rush against each other. Preferences clash. Ideas contend for power and habits vie for position. Sometimes like the waves, they throw up a spray that leaves you breathless and makes you wonder where the loveliness has gone. But that's all right. Like the two rivers, what comes out of their struggle may be something deeper, more powerful than what they were on their own."[1]

I believe two people have the best opportunity for a happy marriage when they have a third Person—the Lord Jesus Christ—working with them and strengthening them. But regardless of the couple's relationship with Christ, they *must* communicate with each other for their marriage to succeed. That's what the rest of this book is all about.

What Causes Misunderstandings?

"But why can't we communicate?"

That's a familiar question, especially for a lot of husbands and wives. But before asking "Why no communication?" we need to take time to ask, "What does communication mean?"

COMMUNICATION IS A PROCESS

There are many definitions of communication. One very good and simple definition is that communication is a process (either verbal or nonverbal) of sharing information with another person in such a way that he understands what you are saying. *Talking, listening,* and *understanding* are all involved in the process of communication.

One of the key problems in communicating is making yourself understood. We often *think* we understand what our mate is saying, but maybe what we heard is not what he or she means at all. In fact, our spouses may not be sure they themselves know what they mean in the first place!

When you stop to think about all that's involved in getting your message across, it's apparent why misunderstandings often occur. Communication specialists point out that when you talk with another person there are actually six messages that can come through.

1. What you mean to say
2. What you actually say
3. What the other person hears
4. What the other person thinks he hears
5. What the other person says about what you said
6. What you think the other person said about what you said

Discouraging? Rather. But it does illustrate why communication is often hard work. We want the other person not only to listen but to understand what we mean. The old proverb, "Say what you mean and mean what you say," is a worthy goal but not an easy one to achieve.

LISTEN MORE, TALK LESS
In his book *Herein Is Love,* Reuel Howe says, "If there is any indispensable insight with which a young married couple should begin their life together, it is that they should try to keep open, at all cost, the

lines of communication between them."[1]

Unfortunately, it is not uncommon for communication lines to be down. Sometimes these breaks in communication are due to the husband and/or wife not being willing or able to talk about what's happening in his or her life. But just as often it is the result of marriage partners not really listening when the other talks. There cannot be strong lines of communication without real listening.

Think about your own communication

pattern. Do you listen? How much of what is said do you hear?

It has been estimated that usually a person hears only about 20 percent of what is said. What is involved in *effective* listening?

Listening effectively means that when someone is talking you are not thinking about what you are going to say when the other person stops. Instead, you are totally tuned in to what the other person is saying. As Paul Tournier says, "How beautiful, how grand and liberating this experience is, when people learn to help each other. It is impossible to overemphasize the immense need humans have to be really listened to."

Listening is more than hearing words. Real listening is receiving and accepting the message as it is sent—seeking to understand what the other person really means. When this happens you can go further than saying, "I hear you." You can say, "I hear what you mean."

While listening is generally regarded as a passive part of communication, this is not true. Sensitive listening is reaching out to the other person, actively caring about what he says and what he wants to say.

In his book *After You've Said I Do,* Dwight Small points out that listening does not come naturally or easily to most people. Most of us do not want to hear as much as we want to speak and to be heard. Because of this we concentrate more on getting our word into the conversation than on giving our attention to what the other person is saying. Also, all too often we filter the other person's remarks through our own opinions and needs.

For example, a wife mentions she's tired of housework. Her husband hears what she says, but the message he receives is that she is unhappy because he isn't providing her with household help like her mother has. That's not what the wife had in mind, but it is what the husband heard. Ever since they were married, it has bothered him that he cannot provide help for the home like his wife's father does. It is easy to see how the message came through differently than the wife intended. Filtered messages are almost never accurate and often cause much misunderstanding.[2]

When both husband and wife recognize the importance of listening objectively and giving each other full attention, they are taking big steps toward building strong lines of communication.

THE POWER OF WORDS

Children attending school soon learn to chant the singsong poem, "Sticks and stones may break my bones, but words will never hurt me." Experience quickly teaches that this is untrue. Words can and do hurt a person.

The Bible recognizes this and talks about word power in both the Old and

13

New Testaments. Proverbs 18:21 states what many have discovered: "Death and life are in the power of the tongue" (NASB). Proverbs 26:22 also speaks of how words really get to a person: "The words of a

14

❏ Yes
❏ No
❏ Sometimes

5. If you feel it would take too much time and effort to understand something, do you go out of your way to avoid hearing about it?
   ❏ Yes
   ❏ No
   ❏ Sometimes

6. When your mate talks to you, do you try to make him or her think you are paying attention when you are not?
   ❏ Yes
   ❏ No
   ❏ Sometimes

7. When you are listening to the other person, are you easily distracted by outside sights and sounds (such as the TV set)?
   ❏ Yes
   ❏ No
   ❏ Sometimes

Look back over your answers. Do they give you clues for improving your listening attitudes and skills?

whisperer . . . go down to the innermost parts of the body" (NASB). This was what Job was experiencing when he cried in frustration, "How long will you torment me, and crush me with words?" (NASB). Or as *The Living Bible* puts it, "How long are you going to trouble me, and try to break me with your words?" (Job 19:2).

James 3:2-10 adds a helpful perspective.

> If anyone can control his tongue, it proves that he has perfect control over himself in every other way. We can make a large horse turn around and go wherever we want by means of a small bit in his mouth. And a tiny rudder makes a huge ship turn wherever the pilot wants it to go, even though the winds are strong.
>
> So also the tongue is a small thing, but what enormous damage it can do.
>
> Men have trained, or can train, every kind of animal or bird that lives and every kind of reptile and fish, but no human being can tame the tongue. It is always ready to pour out its deadly poison. Sometimes it praises our heavenly Father, and sometimes it breaks out into curses against men who are made like God. And so blessing and cursing come pouring out of the same mouth. Dear brothers, surely this is not right!

James likened the power of the tongue to the rudder of a ship. A rudder is a small part of the ship, yet it can turn the ship in any direction and control its destiny. Likewise, what husbands and wives say to one another can turn their marriage in different directions and, in some cases, cause them to wind up going in a vicious circle.

As James wrote, our ingenuity has succeeded in taming almost every kind of living creature; yet we have failed in taming our own tongues! According to the dictionary, "to tame" means "to control" and "to render useful and beneficial." People have not been able to do that with their tongues on any widespread basis.

Each person must be responsible for his own tongue-training program. Controlling the tongue needs to be a continuous goal for every husband and wife because *everything* that is said either helps or hinders, heals or scars, builds up or tears down.

TO UNDERSTAND—COMMUNICATE!

In his book, *The Art of Understanding Your Mate,* Cecil Osborne suggests several ways in which men and women frustrate one another in the marriage relationship.

For example, some women frustrate their husbands by "taking over" and assuming dominance or by becoming emotional in a discussion. Men are also frustrated when women refuse to abandon the romantic dreams of girlhood.

On the other hand, men frustrate their wives by failing to understand the somewhat volatile emotions of their wives. Some women have strong mood swings and may be depressed or made happy by events that do not deeply affect a man. Many a woman is also frustrated when her man fails to understand that "little things," as he sees them, are often "big things" to her. For instance, activities that do not include her, like sports, certain hobbies, and even work, may become sources of

---

WHAT'S YOUR PLAN?
If you are reading this book with your spouse, best results can be obtained if you complete the following material individually and then discuss your answers together.

1. Circle the phrase that you feel describes the quality of communication in your marriage:
   - needs no improvement
   - highly effective
   - satisfactory
   - inconsistent
   - superficial
   - frustrating
   - highly inadequate

   Now go back and put a check mark beside the phrase you think your spouse would choose.

2. List three things *you* can do to improve communication between yourself and your spouse.

   a.

   b.

   c.

frustration to a wife.

But, as Osborne points out, the major source of frustration for wives by their husbands is *that men do not communicate with or listen to their wives.* And, to be fair,

---

"I will start doing these three things (date) _____ *(time)* _____."

3. Make an "appointment" with your mate when you can sit down (perhaps over a cup of coffee) and plan together how you can improve your communication.
(date) _____ *(time)* _____

As you do your planning together be sure to cover the following four points:

a. Share and discuss your responses to question 1 on the quality of communication in your marriage.

b. Share your responses to question 2 on how you plan to improve communication. Ask your mate's opinion to see if he or she feels your suggestion will actually improve communication. If not, work out alternate ideas that both of you approve of.

c. Commit yourself to following your plan for improving communication and stick to it for at least one week.

d. Set a date for one week from now to get together again and evaluate how successful your plan has been. If necessary, revise your plan at that time and repeat the process until you both feel that communication between you is improving.

this can be the case with wives as well.

An additional source of tension is that all too often husbands and wives concentrate on the talking aspect of communication because they are overly concerned about getting their ideas across. In doing this, they fail to listen to the other party. When this happens, husbands and wives have no real idea of what the other is really thinking or feeling. They may talk, but do they really say anything? Or hear anything? Many conversations are dominated with responses like "uh-huh," "Yes," and "I see," and then five minutes later both husband and wife wonder what went on.[3]

Such lack of communication can produce real marriage problems. In fact, many marriage counselors say that the number one problem in marriage is poor communication.

Marriage is an intimate relationship built on mutual understanding, but in order to truly understand another person, you must be able to communicate with him. A husband and wife can know a great deal *about* each other without really knowing one another. Communication is the process that allows people to know each other, to relate to one another, to understand the meaning of the other person's life.

"Why Can't We Talk about It?"

"But I just don't want to talk about it!" Ever hear that from the other half? Ever use it yourself when you are out of patience (or ideas) about what to say next?

There are basic reasons a lot of us can't get through to our spouses or can't be reached by them. And there are basic principles that will help us communicate more effectively.

REASONS FOR NOT COMMUNICATING

Why is it that some people do not communicate?

1. A few people do not have the ability to talk with another person. They have never learned how to share openly with someone else and they have difficulty forming the words.

2. Others are fearful of exposing what they feel or think. They do not want to run

the risk of being rejected or hurt if someone else disagrees with them. This is a protective device. The ability to communicate is not lost when married couples grow apart. It is the desire to communicate that undergoes change. When one or the other no longer wants to be understood or to be understanding, then distance will develop.

3. Others have the attitude that talking won't do any good, so why bother? They are unable to get through to the other person so they stop trying.

4. Some people do not believe that they as a person have anything to offer. They do not think that their ideas are worthwhile. They have a poor self-image and, as a result, they withhold their comments and personal feelings. They have difficulty accepting themselves.

There are times when it is easy to identify the obstacles to good communication. Other times there is a complex mixture of reasons that is hard to pin down. Think back to a situation when you and your spouse couldn't communicate. What was the *real* reason?

FIVE LEVELS OF COMMUNICATION
In his excellent book *Why Am I Afraid to Tell You Who I Am?,* John Powell asserts that we communicate on at least five different levels, from shallow clicheés to deep personal honesty. Fear, apathy, or a

☞ Checkpoint

1. Which reason for not communicating
   applies to you?
   ❑ can't talk to others
   ❑ afraid to expose thoughts
   ❑ feel "why bother?"
   ❑ ideas not worthwhile

2. Which reason for not communicating
   applies to your mate?
   ❑ can't talk to others
   ❑ afraid to expose thoughts
   ❑ feel "why bother?"
   ❑ ideas not worthwhile

3. Maybe you have another reason for
   not wanting to communicate. If so,
   describe it in ten words or less.

poor self-image keep us at the shallow
level, but if we can be freed from our
weaknesses, we can move to deeper, more
meaningful levels.

Powell's five levels of communication
include:

Level Five: Cliché Conversation. This
type of talk is very safe. We use words
such as "How are you?" "How is your family?" "Where have you been?" "I like your
suit." In this type of conversation there is
no personal sharing. Each person remains
safely behind his screen.

Level Four: Reporting the Facts about Others. In this kind of conversation we are content to tell others what someone else has said, but we offer no personal commentary on these facts. We just report the facts like the five o'clock news each day. We share gossip and little narrations but we do not commit ourselves as to how we feel about it.

Level Three: My Ideas and Judgments. This is where real communication begins. The person is willing to step out of his solitary confinement and risk telling some of his ideas and decisions. He is still cautious, however, and if he senses that what he is saying is not being accepted he will retreat.

Level Two: My Feelings or Emotions. Now the person shares how he feels about facts, ideas, and judgments. The feelings underneath these areas are revealed. If a person is to really share himself with another individual, he must get to the level of sharing his feelings.

Level One: Complete Emotional and Personal Truthful Communication. All deep relationships, especially marriage relationships, *must* be based on absolute openness and honesty. This may be difficult to achieve because it involves a risk—the risk of being rejected because of our honesty—but it is vital for relationships to grow. There will be times when this type of communication is achieved and other

☞ Checkpoint

1. On a separate piece of paper, write down subjects or topics you discuss with your spouse at the Level One stage of communication—complete emotional and personal truthful communication.
2. Now write down subjects or topics you do not discuss at Level One.
3. What prevents you from communicating on certain subjects at Level One?
4. What do you think can be done about this? List what you can do to help your partner share more deeply with you.

times when the communication is not as complete as it could be.[1]

These are five suggested levels of communication. Only you know at what level communication is occurring in your marriage. But ask yourself, "What *is* our communication like? On which level are we? How can we move toward Level One in our relationship?"

TWO KEYS TO COMPLETE COMMUNICATION
What is it that really frees a person to open his life to another, to reach out to share and to love another person?

Before we can love someone, we must

have had two basic experiences in our lives. First, we must have experienced love from someone else, and second, we must also love ourselves. But what if we grew up never having experienced the true, unconditional love that is necessary for us to begin loving ourselves? How can one begin to love others and himself when he's an adult? Is it really possible or are we just fooling ourselves?

We find that it is possible to experience this unconditional love from Jesus Christ. John, often called the apostle of love, puts it this way:

> By this the love of God was manifested in us, that God has sent His only begotten Son into the world so that we might live through Him. In this is love, not that we loved God, but that He loved us and sent His Son to be the propitiation for our sins. Beloved, if God so loved us, we also ought to love one another. There is no fear in love; but perfect love casts out fear. . . . We love, because He first loved us. (1 John 4:9-11, 18-19, NASB)

The ability to love yourself and other people is the result of God reaching out and loving you first. When you accept God's forgiveness and acceptance, made possible through Jesus Christ, you experience his love. And as John points out, "There is no fear in love; but perfect love casts out fear" (1 John 4:18, NASB).

So, let it happen. Let God love you his

☞ Checkpoint

Analyze just how much you accept what God has done for you and how he feels about you by completing the following multiple choice statements. Choose answers that match your true feelings.

1. I think of God as
   - ❑ a distant power
   - ❑ my friend
   - ❑ my policeman
   - ❑ my _____

2. When I pray I feel
   - ❑ relaxed and close to God
   - ❑ strained and uncertain
   - ❑ afraid God is displeased with me
   - ❑ _____

3. As a Christian I
   - ❑ try to do better so I will deserve God's love
   - ❑ feel God can't love me the way I act
   - ❑ feel happy because I belong to God's family
   - ❑ _____

4. Describe a lovable person in twenty-five words or less. How would God describe a lovable person? How would he describe an unlovable person? (See John 3:16; Romans 5:8.)

way—with no conditions, no improvements on your part to make yourself "wor-

---

WHAT'S YOUR PLAN?

If you are reading this book with your spouse, best results can be obtained if you complete the following material individually and then discuss your answers together.

Choose three of the following ideas and try them out during the coming week.

1. Decide if there are areas in your relationship with your spouse that could be improved if you would be willing to share how you feel (Level Two communication). Choose one thing that you will talk about with your mate and share your true feelings. Choose a time that's appropriate and honestly tell him or her that you want to share your feelings about something because you believe it would help you feel better.

2. Decide if there are areas in your relationship with God that would be improved if you were willing to tell him how you really feel. (He knows anyway, but he wants *you* to tell him!) Take some time alone this week to tell God your true feelings about yourself and how you feel about him.

3. Discuss with your mate how he or she feels about God. If your feelings do not agree, does this mean that God loves either one of you more than the other? Does your faith in God's acceptance of you "just as you are" help you accept your marriage partner just as he or she is? Can you feel comfortable when your mate has ideas on certain subjects that do not agree with yours?

thy" of God's love. If you try to "shape up" for God and be "worth loving," you play

---

4. Write a letter to God telling him how you feel about his acceptance of you. For ideas read Psalm 103.

5. List ways that you protect yourself or cut yourself off from communicating with your mate. Your list may include things like reading at mealtime; ironing or doing some task that gives you a degree of privacy; turning on TV rather than continuing a conversation; taking a bath so your mate will be asleep when you go to bed. At the end of the week decide which barriers you want to "tear down."

6. Plan a time when you can relax with your husband or wife (when the children are asleep or with a sitter, for example). It should be a time when you are not in a hurry, a time you can enjoy. Perhaps you will want to take a walk, read aloud to each other, share a snack, or just talk about hopes and plans for the future

7. Plan one way that you want to begin to communicate on "Level One" with your husband or wife. Think through what it would mean to really talk about a certain area of your relationship with complete emotional and personal truthfulness. Will talk be enough? What else will you have to do to prepare your husband or wife for your openness? Are there things you can do to build a credibility bridge that will make your openness meaningful and acceptable?

the same game with him that you play with others—especially your mate. You set a standard of what you think is lovable. When you don't reach it or your mate doesn't reach it, you freeze, clutch, or blow up. Fear casts out, or suppresses, the love you want to have for yourself and others.

DOORWAYS TO COMMUNICATION

As you open up to God, you will discover new ability to open up to others. You will be able to communicate at those deeper levels described earlier in this chapter. It works like this:

1. Christ accepts us.
2. We accept Christ's love.
3. We accept ourselves.
4. We accept others.
5. We communicate!

Christ's love and acceptance of us gives us the confidence to share ourselves with others. He accepts us with our failures and defects and sees the great potential that lies within us. Because God accepts us, we can learn to accept ourselves. When we accept ourselves and develop a better self-image, we learn to accept others which leads to a willingness to communicate with those around us. Jesus Christ provides the way for a person to move to the first level of communication!

Anger: Is It Always Off-limits?

Most couples want to communicate with one another. Communication is vitally important when one or both of the partners is angry. Yet anger is one of the main causes of the breakdown of communication in marriage.

Have you ever tried to define the feeling of anger or hostility? Perhaps the simplest definition is a *strong emotion of displeasure.* Emotions generate energy within us. Anger generates energy that impels us to hurt or destroy that which angers us. Anger is the natural, reflexive result of frustration—our reaction to having a goal blocked.

THE PROS AND CONS OF ANGER
Too often we think negatively of anger. But anger also has its positive points. For example, one of our built-in goals is survival. When it appears that goal is

threatened, the frustration resulting from a blocked goal makes us angry. This emotion can spur us on to almost impossible feats in order to survive.

Many of us desire to see justice and righteousness prevail. When this goal is not reached, we become angry. And that is a good thing. When we see injustices around us—other people being hurt or taken advantage of—or when we see suffering, we become angry because these conditions should not be so! The energy produced by this anger can motivate us to correct the injustices.

Of course, we do not always become angry for such noble reasons. Often our anger results from concern for ourselves; we are selfish. We do not get our own way, so we become angry. We make plans, our mate does not agree with them or refuses to cooperate, and we become angry.

"But I've already made reservations at the mountain resort," he states.

"You know how my allergy reacts to that pollen," she retorts. "I want to go to the beach."

"Yeah, but I *always* get sunburned at the beach. Why can't you take your allergy pills?" he questions.

"For the same reason you don't use suntan lotion," she jabs.

And so it goes.

Anger often produces behavior that prevents communication between husband and wife. We can describe such communication-shattering behavior with a variety of words: wound, damage, despise, ridicule, tease, get even, laugh at, shame, criticize, scold, humble, irritate, beat up, crush, and bully. When we find our feelings or actions described by any of these terms, we should stop kidding ourselves. We are angry. Face that fact so that it can be dealt with.

THE BIBLE ON ANGER
What does the Bible say about anger? It gives us several directives and thoughts about this emotion.

First, the Bible says to put some kinds of anger away. "Let all bitterness and indignation and wrath (passion, rage, bad temper) and resentment (anger, animosity) and quarreling (brawling, clamor, contention) and slander (evil-speaking, abusive, or blasphemous language) be banished from you, with all malice (spite, ill will, or baseness of any kind)" (Ephesians 4:31, Amplified). In this verse, Paul referred to anger as a turbulent emotion, the boiling agitation of the feelings. It is passion boiling up within us.

The Christian is also to put away the anger that is abiding and habitual, the kind of anger that seeks revenge: "But now put away and rid yourselves [completely] of all these things: anger, rage, bad feeling toward others, curses and slander and foulmouthed abuse and shameful utterances from your lips!" (Colossians 3:8, Amplified).

The Bible directs us to be "slow to anger" (Proverbs 16:32)—that is, to control our anger—and to be careful of close association with others who are constantly angry or hostile. "Make no friendships with a man given to anger, and with a wrathful man do not associate, lest you learn his ways and get yourself into a snare" (Proverbs 22:24-25, Amplified).

HOW WE RESPOND TO ANGER

How do people react when they are angry—especially in the husband-wife relationship? Most of us choose from at least four basic reactions.

1. *We suppress anger.* Suppressing anger is like building a fence around it. You recognize you are angry and consciously try to keep your anger under control instead of letting your bad feelings spill out in uncontrolled actions or words.

If you can listen to what's going on and hold back long enough to think about what you are going to say, you can usually control your anger in a healthy way. As Dr. William Menninger says, "Do not talk when angry but after you have calmed down."[1]

It is important, however, to eventually talk about your anger. Somewhere, somehow, the anger has to be recognized and released in a healthy manner. Otherwise your storage apparatus will begin to over-flow at the wrong time and in the wrong place.

2. *We express anger.* The opposite reaction to suppressing anger is expressing it. Anger is a strong emotion and it needs expression in some way. Some people go so far as to advocate cutting loose and saying exactly how you feel, when you feel it, no matter how much damage you do.

Granted, expressing anger with violent passion, yelling, sharp words, and high emotions does get results, but the results are usually not too positive. We like to say that we feel better because we "got it off our chest," but chances are neither you nor the people you blast really profit from your anger. Waiting until you've cooled off is better for all concerned.

This doesn't mean you shouldn't express anger in some way. Some people learn to express their anger by redirecting it. They get busy doing something that gives them time to cool off and use up some of the emotional energy they've generated by becoming angry. Some people go outside and cut the grass or dig in the garden. Some walk around the block and others ride a bicycle. Others find it helpful to sit down and write out exactly how they feel. Scrubbing a floor, washing a car, or doing anything that takes physical effort can be a good way of working out the strong, pent-up feelings of anger. Whatever helps you calm down and

☞ Checkpoint

1. What is your usual response when you get angry?
   - ❑ Suppress
   - ❑ Express
   - ❑ Repress
   - ❑ Confess

2. Do you agree with John Powell when he says, "When I repress my emotions my stomach keeps score"? What are other possible ways that repressed anger seems to affect you? Does it make you irritable? Critical? Touchy? Would you say you are aware that you sometimes repress anger and don't want to admit you are angry?

3. Does confessing anger seem like a real possibility for you? That is, is it something you do easily or think you could start doing? What would people say if you were honest and let them know when they were making you angry?

My spouse would say:

My friends would say:

My boss would say:

control your feelings is a good course of action for you as long as it does not hurt others or damage their property.

3. *We repress anger.* The person who represses anger refuses to accept the fact that he is angry.

Many people practice repression, thinking they are not supposed to become angry, that anger is not a legitimate emotion for them. Therefore, when angry feelings arise, they attempt to ignore them and refuse to accept their presence.

But repressing anger is like taking a wastepaper basket full of paper and putting it in a closet and setting it on fire. True, the fire can burn itself out—or it can set the entire house on fire and burn it down. Actually, ulcers, anxiety, headaches, and depression are common results of repressing anger.

Dr. David Augsburger observed, "Repressed anger hurts and keeps on hurting. If you always deal with it simply by holding it firmly in check or sweeping it under the rug, without any form of release or healing, it can produce rigidity and coldness in personality. . . . Or repressed anger may come out indirectly in critical attitudes, scapegoating, or irritableness."[2]

John Powell summed it up nicely when he said, "When I repress my emotions my stomach keeps score."[3]

The point is this. Admitting the presence of anger is a healthy way to respond

37

to anger. Ignoring your anger and repressing your feelings only makes matters worse. Getting angry is not necessarily a sin, but repression of anger is always a sin.

4. *We confess anger.* Some people react to anger by recognizing they are getting angry and confessing it before their feelings get out of control.

This is an excellent response to make to your mate when things are getting a little tense. The secret is to confess your anger in a way that your spouse will be able to accept. You might say, "You know, the way the discussion is going I'm starting to get angry. Now I don't want to get angry, and I know you don't want me to get angry, so perhaps we could stop the discussion, start over, and see if I can get my feelings under control."

Whatever you do, don't say, "You're making me angry." This puts your spouse at fault and will put him or her on the defensive. *Always recognize that you are responsible for your own emotional reaction toward another person.* Confessing your anger to the other person simply means that you are willing to admit you have a problem. You might say: "I'm sorry I'm angry. What can I do now so we can work this thing out?" To confess anger is to get it out in the open where you can discuss the cause of the trouble.

This response to anger is difficult for most of us. Often by the time we admit we are angry, it has already become obvious to our spouse, or whomever we are angry with, that we are definitely irritated and uptight. The key is to learn how to confess anger in a way that does not make the other person feel that you are angry with him already!

MAKE THE MOST OF YOUR ANGER
In his book *Be All That You Can Be,* David Augsburger suggests the following ways to make the most of anger.

First, a person must understand that "anger is a vital, valid, natural emotion. As an emotion, it is in itself neither right nor wrong. The rightness or wrongness depends on the way it is released and exercised.

"Be angry, but be aware. You are never more vulnerable than when in anger. Self-control is at an all-time low, reason decreases, common sense usually forsakes you.

"Be angry, but be aware that anger quickly turns bitter, it sours into resentment, hatred, malice, and even violence unless it is controlled by love.

"Be angry, but only to be kind. Only when anger is motivated by love of your brother, by love of what is right for people, by what is called from you by love for God, is it constructive, creative anger.

"Make the most of your anger. Turn it from selfish defensiveness to selfless compassion."[4]

WHAT'S YOUR PLAN?

Use the following questionnaire to evaluate your own attitude toward anger—what being angry does to you and what you do to others when you get angry. After each question write in "yes," "no," or a more accurate response (using as few words as possible).

1. Do you have a temper?

2. Do you control it?

3. Do others know when you are angry?

4. Describe how you feel when angry.

5. Does your anger surge up quickly?

6. Do you hold resentments?

7. Does your anger affect you physically?

8. Have you ever hit someone or something?

9. When was the last time?

10. How do you control your anger?

11. Who taught you?

12. Are others afraid of your anger?

13. Are others afraid of your criticism?

14. What causes your anger or criticism?

15. How often do you get angry?

16. What are you dissatisfied with in life?

17. Do you get mad at people or things?

18. What do you do about your anger?

19. How do you handle anger directed toward you?

20. Do you repress your anger?

21. Do you suppress it?

22. Do you express it or confess it?

23. Do you know of Scriptures that can help you?

24. Do you regularly memorize Scriptures?

25. Do you openly and honestly pray about your emotions?

26. Do you really expect God to help you change your emotions?

27. Do you want to change?

If you are not satisfied with the way you respond to anger, then what are you going to do now to change your attitudes and behavior? Look back over the previous chapter and think of some specific things you can do to change and list them here.

How to Handle Anger—Before It Handles You

Like it or not, anger is a part of life—including married life. In fact, as the previous chapter points out, anger is an emotion given to us by God himself. Our problem is that we don't handle anger very well. We tend to become angry for the wrong reason or we tend to express angry feelings in a hurtful or damaging way rather than trying to help others and ourselves.

HOW CRITICAL ARE YOU?
For example, one "wrong reason" for anger is a critical attitude. The angry, hostile person is almost always a critical person. He attacks other people verbally or subtly. If you constantly dislike what you see in other people you may be this way. When you look for and are overly aware of the faults and weaknesses in others, you

are too critical and hostile. A person with a critical or hostile disposition is not going to be happy and will alienate those about him.

Are you really critical? Ask yourself these questions: Do you spend more time criticizing people in your mind than looking at their strong points? Do others do things that bother you so much that you feel you have to tell them? Do you talk about others in a derogatory manner behind their backs? Do you have standards for others that you can't live up to yourself? Do you pressure others to conform to your standards so you can accept them easier?

These reactions indicate a critical or hostile attitude.

Why are we critical? It gets attention off of us. It may make us feel better at the expense of others. In his *Psychology and Morals,* Dr. J. A. Hadfield writes: "It is literally true that in judging others we are trumpeting abroad our own secret faults. We personalize our unrecognized failings and hate in others the sins to which we are secretly addicted."

He goes on to say that the real reason for our condemnation of certain sins in others is that these same sins are a temptation to ourselves. It is for this very reason that we denounce so vehemently the miserliness, bigotry, or cynicism of others. Whatever fault we are most intolerant of in others is likely to be among our own besetting sins. "Most of our emotions are directed against ourselves," writes Dr. Hadfield. "Allow any man to give free vent to his feelings and then you may, with perfect safety, turn and say: 'Thou are the man.'"[1]

Whenever we find intense prejudice, intolerance, excessive criticism, and cynicism, we are likely to find projection of our feelings into someone else. We are prone to see in others our own undesirable tendencies.

UNHEALTHY REACTIONS TO ANGER

While a critical attitude is a problem for some people, the problem for most of us is expressing angry feelings in a damaging way. Let's suppose you are going through the day and not feeling particularly critical of anyone or anything. But then feelings of anger suddenly (or not so suddenly) well up within. What do you do with them? Are you helpless? Must you blow your top because "that's the way you are?"

That kind of thinking is a cop-out. Anger won't render you "helpless" unless you want it to—unless you secretly enjoy blowing off steam. The truth is, you *do* have a choice about anger. You can react to anger in one of two ways: healthy or unhealthy. First, take a look at unhealthy reactions that will keep you enslaved— and "helplessly" angry.

Be sure to ignore your emotional reac-

tions. Even though you may be angry with your spouse, tell yourself that your angry feelings have nothing to do with the argument anyway. Even better, if you want to compound the problem, convince yourself that you're not getting upset at all. So what if you're perspiring a little; it's probably just warm in the room.

Be sure to keep your anger down in the pit of your stomach where it won't bother your head. Keep everything on an intellectual level, but don't let your spouse know how you feel.

Next, be sure to keep on denying your emotions. Keep telling yourself, "I'm not mad." So what if your stomach is in a knot and you're perspiring profusely. Keep insisting to your mate that you aren't angry at all. Your mate will believe you.

Also, make sure you keep your mind on the argument and how you can get back at your spouse. It's obvious the one with the right moves and bright lines is going to break this whole discussion wide open and come away the winner. And that's what's important, isn't it? Winning the argument? Especially if you are arguing with your spouse, right?

If you really get mad, blame your spouse. Surely it's his (or her) fault! When arguing with your mate, be sure to raise the volume. Find some defect in your spouse and point it out with great precision and accuracy (and a little exaggeration, too, if you can think of it). Very helpful, rational

46

things such as, "It's impossible to discuss anything with you. You're just too arrogant. You never [generalizations like this are good, too] listen. You think you're God, don't you?"

Finally, don't learn from your emotions. Walk out in a huff, take a couple of aspirins, and concentrate on how unreasonable your spouse was, is, and always will be!²

Obviously, the "unhealthy" reactions listed above are a perfect prescription for disaster in a marriage. Unfortunately, these reactions are all too typical with many husbands and wives.

In their book *Learning for Loving,* Robert McFarland and John Burton point out that "few couples have self-sufficient social skills and emotional maturity to fight constructively for the good of their marriage. We believe, consequently, that most couples urgently need to develop skills and increase their emotional strength sufficiently to engage themselves in such encounters. We believe that many couples seek to avoid constructive conflict because one or both of them feel that changes will have to take place if adequate communication occurred between them."³

But in order to do this, couples must be willing to trust each other—to trust one another with their feelings and with their admissions that what they are hearing and feeling hurts or disturbs them. All too often husbands and wives are too proud to admit to each other that they are uncomfortable, angry, or hurt. And the result is a stalemate in communication.

Dwight Small observes, "All communication in an intimate relationship is built upon mutual trust. To confide in another is to be relatively sure, first of all, that a ground of confidence is shared. Mutual trust grows as each partner takes the other into account as a person whose happiness is bound up with his own."[4]

So how about the antidote to all of these unhealthy habits? There is one, if husbands and wives are willing to react to angry feelings in the following *healthy* ways.

HEALTHY REACTIONS TO ANGER

To begin with, be aware of your emotions. Forget the argument momentarily and concentrate on your emotional reactions. What are you feeling? Embarrassment (because her argument sounds better)? Fear ("He's getting nasty—I hope he doesn't hit me")? Superiority ("I'm ahead on points and she knows it")?

Don't be afraid to admit your emotion. Take a good look at yourself and accept the fact that you are angry. If you are honest, you'll admit that it's high voltage anger, not just a "little" irritation or frustration.

Now investigate how the emotion got there. Ask yourself, "Why am I angry?

Why is my spouse getting to me like this?" Try to trace the origin of your emotion. You may come up with a glimpse of some hidden inferiority complex that you've never recognized or a fear or a weakness you didn't want to admit to your spouse.

Share your emotions with your spouse. Just present the facts with no interpretations or judgments. Say something to your mate such as, "Let's stop. I'm saying things I really don't mean, and I don't want this to happen." Whatever you do, don't judge or accuse your spouse. It isn't your spouse's fault that you are angry. Don't blame your spouse, even to yourself.

Decide what to do with your emotion. What's the best thing to do next? Perhaps you will want to tell your spouse, "Let's start again. I think I've been too defensive to listen to you. I'd like to try it again." Or, if necessary, "Would you mind if we dropped the subject? I'm afraid I'm too touchy to discuss it further right now." (Keep in mind, however, that you had better come back to it later or the problem will continue to grow and rankle the two of you.)

In *Conjoint Family Therapy,* Virginia Satir echoes many of the above ideas. She says, "A person who communicates in a functional (healthy) way can (a) firmly state his case, (b) yet at the same time clarify and qualify what he says, (c) always ask for feedback, (d) and be receptive to feedback when he gets it."[5]

49

Some other ideas for dealing with an emotional situation in a healthy way are offered by Howard and Charlotte Clinebell in their book *The Intimate Marriage:* "A couple may find it helpful to ask themselves questions such as these: Is this really an issue worth fighting over, or is my self-esteem threatened by something my spouse has said or done? In relation to this issue or problem area, what do I want and what does my partner want that we are not getting? What must I give in the relationship in order to satisfy the needs of my partner in this area? What small next step can we take right now toward implementing this decision, made jointly through the give-and-take of discussion?"[6]

TEN STEPS FOR HANDLING ANGER

It helps to know what anger is, what causes anger, how to respond to anger, and so forth. But what finally counts is what you *do* with angry feelings when *you* have them. As a summary to these two chapters on anger, here are ten practical principles for facing angry feelings and controlling them.

Keep in mind, of course, that a person who follows Jesus Christ does not control anger (or any other problem) entirely in his own strength. He relies on God to give him power. And never is God needed more than when a person feels himself getting good and angry!

☞ Checkpoint

"You are having a discussion with your mate. There are several noticeable differences of opinion. Soon voices and emotions begin to rise. You are starting to have some strong feelings toward what is going on and toward the other person. What should you do at this point?"

Describe how to deal with the above situation in an *unhealthy* manner:

Now write a dialogue of two people dealing with the situation in a *healthy* manner.

He:

She:

He:

She:

1. Be aware of your emotional reactions. Ask yourself, "What am I feeling?"

2. Recognize your emotions and admit that you have them. Admitting the feeling

of anger does not mean that you have to act it out.

3. Try to understand why you have anger. What brought it about?

As we mentioned in the last chapter, we are often angry because we are frustrated. We suffer from frustration of our desires, impulses, wants, ambitions, hopes, drives, hunger, or will. When you are getting angry, ask yourself, "Does my anger come from frustration?" Then ask yourself, "What type of frustration?" Next, ask, "What or who is the cause of my frustration?" Ask yourself, "What positive solution can I think of?"

Other reasons why we get angry include:

- The possibility of harm—physical harm or emotional harm. Our security is threatened and as a defense we become angry.
- Injustice—to others, ourselves, or society. Often this can be a "noble kind of anger," which is justified. But be careful and don't allow your righteous indignation over injustice to become confused with another basic cause of anger—selfishness, the major cause of anger in most of us.

4. Can you create other situations in which anger won't occur? What did you do to cause the other person to react in such a way that you became angry?

5. Is anger the best response? Write

down the consequences of your getting angry. What is a better response? What would kindness, sympathy, and understanding of the other person accomplish? Can you confess your feelings to him?

6. Is your anger the kind that rises too soon? If so, take some deep breaths or count to ten. Concentrate on the strengths and positive qualities of the other person instead of his defects.

7. Do you find yourself being critical of others? What does this do for you?

Be less suspicious of other persons. Listen to what they say and feel. Evaluate their comments instead of condemning them. They may have something to offer to you.

Does your criticalness or anger come from a desire to make yourself feel better? Are your opinions always accurate or could they be improved?

Slow down in your speech and reactions toward others. Watch your gestures and expressions as they may convey rejection and criticism of the other person. Can you express appreciation and praise of the other in place of criticism?

8. You may have a time when your anger or criticism is legitimate. When you express it, plan ahead and do it in such a way that the other person can accept what you say. Use timing and tact and have a desire to help the other person instead of tearing him or her down.

9. Find a friend with whom you can talk

over your feelings and gain insight from his suggestions. Admit how you feel and ask for his guidance.

10. Spend time praying for the difficulty that you have with your feelings. Openly admit your situation to God. Ask for his

---

WHAT'S YOUR PLAN?

1. On a separate piece of paper, describe the behavior or attitude that you want to change (e.g., anger, anxiety, quarreling, or yelling).

2. List several personal reasons for giving up this behavior or attitude.

3. Motivation to change is very important. From your reasons for giving up the behavior or attitude, select the most important reason. Write it down.

4. Begin to think about how you should change your behavior if you wish to succeed. Write these changes down.

5. Adopt a positive attitude. What has been your attitude toward changing this in the past? Describe it. Indicate what attitude you are going to have now. How will you maintain this new attitude? Write down your answer.

6. Whenever you eliminate a behavior or attitude that you dislike, often a vacuum or void will remain. Frequently, a person prefers the bad or poor behavior to this emptiness, so

help. Memorize Scriptures that speak of anger and of how we should behave toward others. Memorize and understand them and put them into practice.

---

he reverts back to the previous pattern. In order for this not to happen, substitute a positive behavior in place of the negative. Describe what you can substitute for the behavior or attitude that you are giving up.

7. Consider Ephesians 4:31-32: "Let all bitterness and wrath and anger and clamor and slander be put away from you, along with all malice. And be kind to one another, tender-hearted, forgiving each other, just as God in Christ also has forgiven you" (NASB).

List the positive behavior or attitude that this Scripture suggests in place of the negative one you experience. Write out the way you see yourself putting this Scripture into action in your life. Describe specific situations and picture yourself actually doing what the Scriptures suggest. What would be the consequences of thinking or behaving in his new way?

Ten Ways to Cope with Conflict

Sugar-coated myths picture marriage as the time when you "live happily ever after." Fighting and disagreeing, say the myths, are just not part of a healthy marriage.

But the sugarcoating quickly melts away under the heat of reality. Marriage *does* include conflict because a marriage is a union of two individuals who have unique viewpoints, frames of reference, and values. No two people can agree on everything all the time.

UNDERSTANDING CONFLICT

What exactly is conflict? For some the word conjures up scenes of battlegrounds and warfare. This is one of the meanings of conflict, but the meaning with which this chapter is concerned is, according to Webster, "mental struggle resulting from incompatible or opposing needs, drives, wishes, or external or internal demands."

That definition is a challenge for every married couple. How can they handle their disagreements—the tensions that come when the needs and drives of one spouse are at cross-purposes with those of the other? How do they keep cross-purposes from becoming crossed swords?

Every married couple needs to know how to deal with conflict in a creative, constructive way. Objectivity, flexibility, a willingness to compromise (Is squeezing the toothpaste tube at the bottom rather than in the middle *really* one of the big issues of life?), and the willingness to let the other person be himself all need to be developed if couples are to enjoy a satisfying and growing marriage relationship.

When conflict comes, it should be faced with the understanding that disagreements do not mean the entire relationship is on the verge of breaking down. Nor should a disagreement be a trigger for a knockdown, drag-out scrap (verbal and/or physical). Husbands and wives need to know how to "disagree agreeably" or, to put it in a little stronger terms, "fight fair."

Unfortunately, few couples get any training on how to fight fair before marriage. As a result, their disagreements often turn into spats, heated arguments, and quarrels. All of this really isn't necessary. Any couple can cope better with conflict by using the following ten principles.

DON'T USE THE SILENT TREATMENT

Some people use the "silent treatment" as a means of avoiding controversy. They use silence as a weapon to control, frustrate, or manipulate their spouse. Or sometimes the husband or wife takes the pathway of silence because it seems to be the least painful. Perhaps one spouse is silent now because in the past the other spouse was not a ready listener. Also, there's always the possibility of a deep hurt that is keeping one marriage partner silent.

But silence never pays off in the long run. "Silence is golden," so the saying goes, but it can also be yellow! Don't hide behind silence because you are afraid to deal with the issue at hand.

Marriage counselors estimate that at least one half of the cases they see involve a silent husband. Men have a tendency to avoid conflict in discussion. Ironically, the issues they avoid are often the ones that indicate where adjustments and changes need to be made—and fast.

Here is a typical pattern that results in the use of silence. When married partners are not communicating because one of them is silent, both of them experience frustration and a rising sense of futility, all of which compound the silence problem. The more the communicative person tries to talk, the farther the silent person draws into his hostile shell. The person who is trying to talk then feels increasingly useless, inadequate, and hurt. The talkative

59

☞ Checkpoint

1. Check how you *tend* to respond when controversy arises:
   ❏ I talk incessantly.
   ❏ I clam up.
2. On a separate piece of paper, list several reasons you think a person might choose to be silent.
3. When would it be best for you to be silent? Why? Will your silence solve the problem or improve communication in the long run?
4. Write down several things you can do to encourage a silent mate to be more expressive.

spouse may try shouting, even violence, in an attempt to drive the silent mate from his refuge. But this does nothing more than drive the silent spouse into deeper silence. When you say to a silent person, "Why don't you talk to me?" or "Please say something—why can't we communicate?" it usually does nothing more than reinforce that person's silence![1]

How, then, do you encourage the silent person to talk? First, you have to let the silent partner choose the time to speak. Then, when this person does speak, you must communicate in every way you can that you're willing to listen without judging what is said; you are willing to accept feelings and frustrations. The silent person must find that you really do listen and care. If you create an acceptant, unthreatening climate, the silent spouse will in all likelihood start talking. Then communication can begin or be reestablished.

DON'T SAVE "EMOTIONAL TRADING STAMPS"

Always watch yourself to make sure you're not saving up hostility. A husband or wife, for example, could easily save up a lot of hostility when trying to deal with a mate who is dealing out the silent treatment. But the worst method of dealing with feelings of irritation or frustration is to deny them and bottle them up. Feelings must be expressed. They shouldn't be allowed to accumulate.

Some individuals, however, deal with their emotions like trading stamps. They save up each little irritation as though it were a stamp. They accumulate many stamps and, finally, when something happens that is the last straw, they blow up and "cash in" with all of their pent-up irritations and frustrations. Their emotional trading-stamp book becomes full, and they decide that now is the time to trade it in. In this way they think they "get something back" for all of their trouble. They "redeem" their trading stamps, so to speak, and tell themselves, "Well, now at least I feel better."

Are you an emotional stamp saver? If

you suspect you are, now is the time to start doing something about it. It is much better to release your emotions as they *arise*. God created all of us to feel deeply, but we must express what we feel. Our expressions should—and can—be done in a healthy way.

IF POSSIBLE, PREPARE THE SETTING FOR DISAGREEMENT

If you have a major discussion on an important topic coming up with your spouse, try to arrange for the best time and place for both of you. Guard against interruption. You may want to take the phone off the hook or not answer the door. If you have children, ask them not to interrupt you. If the children do interrupt you, let them know that you are having an important discussion and will talk to them when you are finished.

Parents do not usually succeed in hiding disagreements and arguments from their children. Let your kids know that you do disagree sometimes and that all family members will have times of disagreement. Keep in mind that your children will learn their pattern for disagreeing and arguing from watching you. If you can establish healthy patterns for disagreement with your spouse, it can do a lot to help your children learn to disagree in a healthy way—all of which can add to peace and harmony around the house.

How do *you* handle your disagreements?
Ask yourself these questions:
- Am I really being hurt or affected by this?
- Will counter-anger, even if it's justified and rational, really help here?
- Is getting angry the most effective thing I can do?
- What will my anger accomplish?
- How do I respond to or answer another person who is angry?

ATTACK THE PROBLEM, NOT EACH OTHER

Do your best to keep the discussion impersonal. Instead of attacking the problem, too many couples attack each other with innuendoes, slurs, and other "smart" remarks.

There is an old story about a sheepherder in Wyoming who would observe the behavior of wild animals during the winter. Packs of wolves, for example, would sweep into the valley and attack the bands of wild horses. The horses would form a circle with their heads at the center of the circle and kick out at the wolves, driving them away. Then the sheepherder saw the wolves attack a band of wild jackasses. The animals also formed a circle, but they formed it with their heads out toward the wolves. When they began to kick, they ended up kicking one another.

People have a choice between being as smart as a wild horse or as stupid as a wild jackass. They can kick the problem or they can kick one another. Here are five tips to help you kick the problem—to disagree without kicking your spouse:

1. *Back up any accusation or statement you make with facts.*

2. *Stay in the present.* Complaints over six months old are not permissible. Avoid saying, "I remember when. . . ." There is a sign over one businessman's desk that reads, "Remember to Forget." Every couple needs to place that very sign over their marriage.

3. *Do not make references to relatives or in-laws.*

4. *Do not make references to your mate's appearance.* That is, refrain from injecting jabs and cutting remarks about overweight, falling hair, sloppy clothes, etc.

5. *No dramatics, please.* No getting highly emotional and exploding into tears. Crying is often a means of manipulating the other person. Threats are also used for manipulation. Some spouses even threaten suicide as an attempt to control their mates. But none of these methods works. There are no Oscars for dramatics when married people are trying to work out a disagreement.

☞ Checkpoint

What if your spouse attacks you instead of the problem?

1. If an accusation or statement is made that is not backed up with facts, I will say . . .

2. When a complaint that is over six months old is raised, I will state . . .

3. If a reference is made to an in-law or relative, I will . . .

4. If I make a reference to my mate's appearance, I will . . .

5. If a reference is made to my appearance, I will . . .

6. When either I or my mate becomes "dramatic," I will . . .

Review your answers to these six situations. Are your answers positive or negative? Will they help or hurt your mate? Will they make communication more effective next time or will they tend to hinder it? If your answers are negative, hurtful, or may hinder future communication, rewrite them!

DON'T "THROW YOUR FEELINGS" AT YOUR SPOUSE

Learn how to inform your spouse of your feelings. Don't hurl them like a spear or a rock.

Dr. Howard Clinebell suggests that a "road to productive communication is for both husband and wife to learn the skill of *saying it straight*. Each person can help the other to understand by asking himself, 'Am I saying what I really mean?' This involves learning to be aware of what one is actually feeling and developing the ability to put the feeling clearly into words. Direct rather than devious, specific rather than generalized statements are required.

"A wife criticizes her husband as he sits at the breakfast table hidden behind his newspaper. 'I wish you wouldn't always slurp your coffee.' What she really means is, 'I feel hurt when you hide in the newspaper instead of talking to me.' Saying it straight involves being honest about negative as well as positive feelings and being able to state them in a nonattacking way: 'I feel . . . ,' rather than 'You are . . .' Some risk is required in the beginning of this kind of communication until both husband and wife can trust the relationship enough to be able to say what they really mean.

"James Farmer tells a story about a woman who acquired wealth and decided to have a book written about her genealogy. The well-known author she engaged for the assignment discovered that one of her grandfathers had been electrocuted in Sing Sing. When he said it would have to be included in the book, she pleaded for a way of saying it that would hide the truth. When the book appeared, it read as follows: 'One of her grandfathers occupied the chair of applied electricity in one of America's best-known institutions. He was very much attached to his position and literally died in the harness.' The meaning in some attempts to communicate between marriage partners is almost as hidden and confusing. It is usually better to 'say it like it is,' gently if necessary, but clearly."[2]

STAY ON THE SUBJECT
Always try to discover exactly what you are arguing about and stay on that subject. Don't bring in matters that are irrelevant or unimportant.

At times you may have to say something like, "Let's stop this conversation and really see what it is we're talking about. You start again and I will listen. Perhaps I have misunderstood something." Take the initiative to do this yourself. Don't wait for your spouse to do so. Always be willing to listen and ask questions.

OFFER SOLUTIONS
WITH CRITICISMS

If you criticize your spouse, can you offer a clear-cut solution at the same time? To say, "The way you leave your dirty clothes lying around makes our bedroom look like a pigpen" really doesn't help. Saying, "Would it help keep our bedroom neater if I moved the clothes hamper into the bedroom so we wouldn't have to walk so far?" offers a solution to the problem and also communicates displeasure with the status quo.

As you are engaging in an argument or an important discussion, remember to ask yourself, "Is there really as much of a problem or difference of opinion here as I think? Am I seeking a real solution or just looking for problems?"

A clue to your habitual responses to your spouse may lie in whether you are an optimist or a pessimist. The difference is easy to see in this old but still humorous story:

"There were two farmers. One was a pessimist, the other was an optimist.

"The optimist would say, 'Wonderful sunshine.'

"The pessimist would respond, 'Yeah, I'm afraid it's going to scorch the crops.'

"The optimist would say, 'Fine rain.'

"The pessimist would respond, 'Yeah, I'm afraid we are going to have a flood.'

"One day the optimist said to the pessimist, 'Have you seen my new bird dog?

He's the finest money can buy.'

"The pessimist said, 'You mean that mutt I saw penned up behind your house? He don't look like much to me.'

"The optimist said, 'How about going hunting with me tomorrow?' The pessimist agreed. They went. They shot some ducks. The ducks landed on the pond. The optimist ordered his dog to get the ducks. The dog obediently responded. Instead of swimming in the water after the ducks, the dog walked on top of the water, retrieved the ducks, and walked back on top of the water.

"The optimist turned to the pessimist and said, 'Now what do you think of that?'

"Whereupon the pessimist replied, 'Hmmm, he can't swim, can he?'"[3]

Aren't we all like that at times? We can't see the good or the strong points of our spouse because we focus on faults or problems. Perhaps it wouldn't hurt for every husband and wife to memorize Philippians 4:8-9: "Fix your thoughts on what is true and good and right. Think about things that are pure and lovely, and dwell on the fine, good things in others. Think about all you can praise God for and be glad about. Keep putting into practice all you learned from me and saw me doing, and the God of peace will be with you."

NEVER SAY, "YOU NEVER ..."

There's nothing like a sweeping statement or a vast generalization to increase the difficulty of communication. Avoid words like "never," "always," "all," and "everyone." Avoid loaded statements such as: "You're never on time"; "You're always saying things like that"; "All women are emotional"; "All men are like that"; "Everyone thinks you are that way, and so do I!"

Two other excellent ways to decrease difficulty in a conversation are these: Watch your volume, and don't exaggerate.

Most of us tend to raise our voices during family discussions. When we do this, we are really saying, "I can't get through to you in a normal voice because you seem to be deaf to what I say. So I will turn up the volume." Raising our voice puts our spouse on the defensive and can even convey that we have lost control of our temper or of the situation.

It's easy to add to your problems by exaggerating. We seem to think the facts as they are do not make any impression upon our spouse, so we try to get our spouse's attention by altering the facts or "dressing them up a little bit." The sweeping generalization is a typical way that we exaggerate.

She says, "You never finish anything you start around here. You've been working on that fence for the last six months!"

He says, "You're always late. You make us late when we go out to dinner, to the theatre, to PTA, to church. We're going to be late for our funeral!"

A verse from Ephesians contains good advice for spouses who exaggerate: "lovingly follow the truth at all times— speaking truly, dealing truly, living truly— and so become more and more in every way like Christ" (Ephesians 4:15).

DON'T USE CRITICISM TO BECOME A COMEDIAN
While it's true that a joke or dry remark might relieve the tension in some marital disagreements, it's always best to use humor with care. Never try to be funny by criticizing your spouse. The problem might not be serious to you, but it might be very important to your mate.

Questions to ask before using humor are:

- "Will this increase tension or relieve it?"
- "Can I laugh at myself, or am I just trying to poke fun at my mate?"
- "Am I trying to win points for my side with cute remarks?"

WHEN YOU'RE WRONG, ADMIT IT; WHEN YOU'RE RIGHT, SHUT UP
Have the humility to remember that you could be wrong. A lot of people find this sentence difficult if not impossible to say: "I'm wrong; you may be right." Practice

saying it by yourself if necessary, and then be able to say it when it fits into a disagreement or discussion. When you honestly own up to knowing that you're wrong and the other person is right, you improve communication a thousandfold and deepen your relationship with your spouse.

And when it is appropriate, always ask for forgiveness. Proverbs 28:13 has good advice: "A man who refuses to admit his mistakes can never be successful. But if he confesses and forsakes them, he gets another chance." Say something like, "You know, I do think that I am to blame here. I'm sorry I said that and that I hurt you. What can I do now to help or make up for this?"

And when your spouse confesses faults or admits error, be sure to tell him or her of your forgiveness. Even if you were right, take the initiative to forgive *and forget.* Proverbs 17:9 teaches, "Love forgets mistakes."

In summary, Ogden Nash once gave this word to husbands (which also is certainly appropriate for wives):

To keep your marriage brimming
with love in the loving cup,
When you're wrong, admit it;
when you're right, shut up.

WHAT'S YOUR PLAN?

Reprinted below are the "Ten Principles for Coping with Conflict." Review them and check off the ones where you feel fairly strong and capable. Go over them again and underline the ones where you feel weak—in need of more practice.

❑ Don't use the silent treatment.
❑ Don't save "emotional trading stamps."
❑ If possible, prepare the setting for disagreement.
❑ Attack the problem, not each other.
❑ Don't throw your feelings like stones.
❑ Stay on the subject.
❑ Offer solutions with your criticisms.
❑ Never say, "You never . . ."
❑ Don't misuse humor.
❑ Be humble—you could be wrong.

Get together with your mate and share your findings from reviewing the above. (A word of caution: Apply the principles to *yourself*. Don't infer that "A lot of these are really *your mate's* problem," or you may wind up in a disagreement (conflict) over this chapter on coping with conflict. If you do get into a disagreement, be sure to use the Ten Principles and "fight fair!" Good luck!)

CHAPTER 6

Communicate to Build Self-Esteem

An important key to communication—perhaps *the* key—is self-esteem. A person's self-esteem is his overall judgment of himself—how much he likes himself. High self-esteem doesn't mean you are on a continual ego-trip. High self-esteem means you have solid feelings of self-respect and self-worth. You are glad you are you.[1]

Marriage partners with high self-esteem are bound to be happier and communicate better. High self-esteem means an absence or at least a considerable lessening of anxieties, complexes, hang-ups, and the other problems that prevent good communication. The spouse with low self-esteem is seldom a good communicator. Low self-esteem often drives a person into a shell of silence or compels a person to become a dominating, overtalkative, unacceptant dictator in one-way communication—*"my way."*

This final chapter is dedicated to the

continuing challenge of building your mate's self-esteem—making him or her feel important, wanted, valuable, successful, and above all, loved. Following are ten practical ways to build self-esteem in your mate.

MAKE IT SAFE TO COMMUNICATE

Strive to establish and maintain an open, permissive atmosphere in your home. In a permissive atmosphere, both marriage partners are free to share honestly and lovingly what they feel, think, and believe. The husband or the wife does not consciously erect barriers to communication with his or her mate.

Sometimes a spouse tells his mate, "I didn't tell you that because I was afraid of hurting you." We can all think of situations in which speaking the truth will hurt our marriage partner. But does lying really avoid unpleasantness in the long run? Lies—even gentle white lies told to keep the peace—have a way of being discovered, and when they are discovered there is even more unpleasantness.

When you consider lying to avoid unpleasantness, you should be brutally honest with your motivation. Are you really afraid of hurting your spouse? Or is it yourself that you're worried about? Are you just trying to ease out of an unpleasant situation because it isn't worth the hassle? Too often, marriage partners avoid con-

structive discussions because they feel
they would have to make changes in their
own lives if any communication would
take place on that level.

SEEK TO UNDERSTAND,
NOT TO BE UNDERSTOOD

Spend as much time and effort trying to
understand your mate's viewpoint as you
do trying to make him or her understand
yours. Perhaps there's a good reason for
your spouse's beliefs, actions, or habits.
Everyone's background and environment
is different, and each person brings this
background into the marriage relationship.

Paul Tournier wrote:

You well know that beautiful prayer of
Francis of Assisi: 'Lord! Grant that I may
seek more to understand than to be understood. . . .' It is this new desire which
the Holy Spirit awakens in couples and
which transforms their marriage. As
long as a man is preoccupied primarily
with being understood by his wife, he is
miserable, overcome with self-pity, the
spirit of demanding, and bitter
withdrawal. As soon as he becomes
preoccupied with understanding her,
seeking to understand that which he
had not before understood, and with his
own wrongdoing in not having understood her, then the direction taken by
events begins to change. As soon as a
person feels understood, he opens up

and because he lowers his defenses he is also able to make himself better understood.[3]

Tournier felt so strongly about the need for understanding one another that he said the husband and wife should become *preoccupied* with it—lost in it—engrossed to the fullest in learning what makes the other one tick, what the other one likes, dislikes, fears, worries about, dreams of, believes in, and *why* he or she feels this way.

As is so often the case, Scripture has taught this kind of basic truth for centuries. Long ago the Apostle Paul directed the Ephesians to live in a becoming way, "with complete lowliness of mind (humility) and meekness (unselfishness, gentleness, mildness), with patience, bearing with one another and making allowances because you love one another" (Ephesians 4:2, Amplified).

The cry "You don't understand!" is the childish whine of an immature mate who is playing games with his or her marriage partner. The prayer of St. Francis, "Lord! Grant that I may seek more to understand than to be understood," is the honest plea of the husband or wife who wants to communicate—who wants to build a sound and successful marriage by building up the other partner.

🖙 Checkpoint

1. On a separate piece of paper, jot down what you think your mate believes about each of these subjects:
   - The role of the husband
   - The role of the father
   - The role of the wife
   - The role of the mother
   - Male and female tasks in the home
   - Politics
   - Women's lib
   - Sex
   - The importance of a creative outlet for the husband
   - The importance of a creative outlet for the wife
   - Recreation together as a couple/family
2. Now compare notes with your spouse and discuss what you assumed and what is actual fact.

DON'T ASSUME YOU KNOW—ASK

Recognize there is some information you cannot get by any other means than asking your spouse about it. Never assume you know what your spouse thinks. Have you ever heard a husband saying, "My wife thinks . . ."? How does he know? Does he *really* know she thinks or believes that? Or is he just taking it for granted? Has he asked her? Has he ever discussed the matter?

Assumptions about what your spouse

knows, thinks, or feels are dangerous. True, it is easy to get impressions about what people believe from the nonverbal language they use—their looks, glances, and mannerisms. But if you really want to know what your spouse is thinking, start talking about it. Husband-wife communication will automatically improve if both stop assuming and start communicating. Some night soon (or right now) turn off the tube and talk together using the ideas in the box on page 82.

PAUSE TO LISTEN!
Much has been said in earlier chapters about listening, but enough can't be said about this skill.

It may well be true that the first duty of love is to listen. Dr. S. S. Hayakawa says, "We can, if we are able to listen as well as to speak, become better informed and wiser as we grow older, instead of being stuck like some people with the same little bundle of prejudices at sixty-five that we had at twenty-five."

But listening takes discipline. We fail to listen to our spouse because of impatience and a lack of concentration, especially when he or she is saying something we don't particularly want to hear.

Perhaps it is hardest to listen when your spouse picks a poor time to bring something up. For example, you come home late at night, exhausted, and your spouse is already in bed asleep (or so you think). You get ready for bed, wearily crawl in, and are just ready for dreamland when, all of a sudden, you find out your spouse isn't sleeping at all. She's been waiting for you and she says, "I'd like to talk to you about something that's been bothering me quite a bit."

Your initial reaction might well be, "Of all the dumb times to bring up something. Why doesn't she do it during the day and not at this ridiculous hour? Can't she see that it's late and I'm beat?"

Granted, this kind of timing is hardly the best, but before you plead to "Let's talk about it tomorrow," think it through. Why has she waited so long to bring something up? Why wait until you're both in bed and it's easy to hide in the darkness? Could there be something you might have done to make it difficult for your partner to talk about what is on her mind? Consider these questions before you react. You might learn something if you pause to listen!

TOO MUCH TALKING
When trying to communicate with your mate, keep in mind the ironic fact that too much talking can be as bad as too little. If you have adequately discussed a problem or a subject, drop it and move on. Do not restate your case and your conclusions over and over again.

A typical form of "too much talking" is

☞ Checkpoint

During the next few days, try the following experiment.

Spend thirty minutes alone with your spouse and set aside everything else. First, the wife has five minutes in which she will talk about anything she wants to. During that five minutes the husband must listen—he cannot talk—and he must try to think of nothing except what his wife is saying to him. He should not try to daydream or think of what he would like to say in return.

At the end of five minutes, switch roles. Now the husband talks and the wife listens.

Switch back and forth every five minutes so that each spouse has at least three opportunities to talk and three opportunities to listen.

At the end of thirty minutes, discuss your reactions and thoughts concerning this kind of activity. How can you apply this experience to your usual pattern of communicating?

nagging—constantly harping or hassling your mate for one reason or another. A technical definition is "critical faulting"— but whatever you call it, nagging usually doesn't work. It irritates and frustrates both marriage partners—the nagger as well as the "naggee."

You may have heard the quip, "The wife who uses good horse sense never turns out to be a nag." According to a national survey conducted by a leading magazine, the thing that irritates most men more than anything else is the wife's nagging.

On the other hand, men nag just as much as women. You may have said something like this yourself recently: "Nagging is the only way I know of to get my spouse to respond. And it's the same with the kids. If I don't tell them a dozen times, the job never gets done!"

It's true that spouses and children especially seem to "need to be nagged." But perhaps there is a better way. Consider the possibility that you may have conditioned your spouse and your children not to respond to you unless you nag—repeat and repeat and increase the volume as you do so.

How then can you gain your spouse's attention and not have to repeat yourself? Perhaps your husband is watching the tube and you need to get a message through. Your problem is he's watching the Cowboys and the Redskins, and that's an awful lot of opposition for any message—even yours. Use this simple strategy: Roll out to the left around his recliner, cut straight downfield, and wind up standing right in front of the television set. If you really want to put on the pressure, *turn off* the television set. Your spouse's attention is guaranteed.

Or maybe your wife is engrossed in

planning a big dinner party for Saturday night, and you need to give her the word on servicing the car before you leave for work. The last thing she wants to hear is about what oil needs changing and where the grease has to go. So, go up to her and look her right in the eye as you talk to her. Perhaps you may want to put your hand on her shoulder (better yet, put your arms around her waist) and tell her what you have to say.

There are all kinds of ways—some of them pleasant—to be something else than a nagger. Be creative and experiment.

DON'T JUMP TO CONCLUSIONS

Jumping to conclusions is a favorite sport in just about any setting, but it's particularly easy to do in a marriage.

She says, "Honey, I was out shopping today and I stopped in this cute little dress shop and I had the best time—"

He explodes: "What! You blew a bundle of money on some new clothes? You know we can't afford it!" (Actual situation: She tried on a few dresses and didn't buy a thing.)

Or he says, "Say, I was talking with some of the boys at the office and they're planning to get up this foursome Saturday and I—"

And so she snaps: "You're going golfing when you've got all that trim to paint and the yard is beginning to look like an annex for Jungleland, U.S.A.?" (Actual situation: He turned down the boys at the office because he "had a lot of work to do at home.")

The illustrations go on and on and on. And self-esteem in both marriage partners suffers because of it.

Not only is it important to take your time when you feel yourself going into a "jump to conclusions" crouch, but, on the positive side, it's helpful to take the time to say the right kind of remarks. As Solomon put it, "A word spoken at the right moment, how good it is!" (Proverbs 15:23, Amplified).

The illustrations (and opportunities) are endless as far as marriage is concerned. One obvious area where husbands can't say enough at the right moment is when complimenting their wives' appearance. Instead of waiting for her to pry approval out of you about her hair, dress, cooking, and so forth, take a little more notice of your wife and pay her sincere compliments without having to have them solicited. A compliment coming from a husband—a spontaneous compliment—is worth a hundred times more in self-esteem value than the typical grunt: "Oh, yes . . . looks very nice. . . ."

As for the wives, they should never forget that their husbands are just as vain as they are (and more so). They also like compliments on their appearance, and, again, it's better to do it at a spontaneous moment than to wait till he is just putting on his new suit. All of us have a built-in resistance to compliments when they're given at those times "when a compliment is expected." Learn to give compliments when they're not expected, and they'll be worth much more on the self-esteem market with your mate.

DISAGREE? YES. DISRESPECT? NO!

Always show respect for your mate's opinions even when you disagree. As already mentioned, no husband and wife can agree all of the time. But that doesn't mean they can't respect each other for their opinions and be willing to listen to one another. As Voltaire said, "I disapprove of what you say, but I will defend to the death your right to say it." You may not want to get that oratorical the next time you and your spouse disagree, but whatever you do, don't come up with such typical gems as these:

"You're out to lunch."

"I just can't *believe* you!" (meaning, "I don't question your veracity, just your right to belong to the human race").

"Oh, come on, don't get on that junk again."

A well-known TV comedian gained fame and fortune with the line: "I don't get no respect." Perhaps one reason for his

☞ Checkpoint

1. Think of several instances in which you showed respect for your spouse's ideas, opinions, or beliefs in the last week:

2. Think of several instances in which you may have shown disrespect for your spouse's opinions or ideas or beliefs in the last week:

3. Talk together with your mate about "respect for each other's opinions." If apologies are in order, make them. If gratitude or compliments are in order because both of you do respect one another, don't hold back on that either!

success is that so many husbands and wives identify completely with the idea of "not getting much respect." Paul must have had husbands and wives particularly in mind when he wrote: "Never act from motives of rivalry or personal vanity, but in humility think more of each other than you do of yourselves. None of you should think only of his own affairs, but consider other people's interests also" (Philippians 2:3-4, Phillips).

DEAL IN POTENTIAL—NOT THE PAST
Don't limit your mate by what he or she has done in the past that hasn't measured

up to or met completely with your approval. Are you guilty of putting your spouse in a pigeonhole? Check yourself and see if you ever (or often) make comments like these:

"She doesn't listen to what I say."

"He just won't change."

"She says one thing and then does another."

"I just can't reach him. . . . He's hopeless."

If you've used any comments like these, ask yourself, "Would my spouse make the same statements about me? Do I do what I accuse my spouse of doing?"

A Christian couple will not stereotype or pigeonhole one another if they remember the key truth from the New Testament: God is far more interested in what a person can be than in what a person has been.

"Do you see other people in the process of becoming something better or do you see them as being bound by their past— what they have (or haven't) done or said (especially to you)? . . . It is easy to stereotype others. You can place them in neat little pigeonholes like 'sloppy,' 'talk too much,' 'dishonest,' 'undependable,' 'unfair,' etc. . . . Christianity, however, deals in *potential,* and what a person can *become,* not only what he *is.*

"This is the heart of the gospel. If God had dealt with us strictly on the basis of our past, he would never have sent Christ to die for our sins. But God loved us. He saw us as persons of worth, value, with potential. He forgave; he keeps on forgiving, always looking forward to what we can become if we respond to the opportunity we have in Christ."[4]

DON'T FORCE YOUR SPOUSE TO BE YOUR CARBON COPY

If you truly love your mate, you will not demand (subtly or otherwise) that he or she become a modified version of your ideas or a revised edition of yourself. Set your mate free to be an individual with his or her own opinions. Always guard against giving your mate the impression that you love him or her more when he or she agrees with you. Keep in mind that ". . . all of us are self-conscious. Our image of self is directly related to how we feel, what we do, things we like. Criticize a person's viewpoint, taste, ideas, and you criticize *him,* no matter how much you may mean otherwise.

"Before turning your guns (especially your spiritual guns) on someone's ideas, attitudes, actions, ask yourself a couple of questions: Am I trying to help this person or am I really trying to impose my value system on him? Do I respect and like this person for what he is, or am I trying to make him over to suit my idea of what is respectable, likable, or spiritual?"[5]

PRAY FOR ONE ANOTHER

Pray for each other privately and, if you can, pray together for each other. To paraphrase a well-known slogan, "If a husband and wife pray together, not only will

---

WHAT'S YOUR PLAN?

Study the following "Marriage Communication Guidelines." Go through each of the ten guidelines and all of the suggested Scripture verses. Talk about each one. Then sign your names to the guidelines and put in the date.

MARRIAGE COMMUNICATION GUIDELINES

1. Be a ready listener and do not answer until the other person has finished talking. (Proverbs 18:13; James 1:19)
2. Be slow to speak. Think first. Don't be hasty in your words. Speak in such a way that the other person can understand and accept what you say. (Proverbs 15:23, 28; 21:23; 29:20; 1 Peter 3:10)
3. Speak the truth always but do it in love. Do not exaggerate. (Ephesians 4:15, 25; Colossians 3:9)
4. Do not use silence to frustrate the other person. Explain why you are hesitant to talk at this time.
5. Do not become involved in quarrels. It is possible to disagree without quarreling. (Proverbs 17:14; 20:3; Romans 13:13; Ephesians 4:31)
6. Do not respond in anger. Use a soft and kind response. (Proverbs 14:29; 15:1; 25:15; 29:11; Ephesians 4:26)

they stay together but they will communicate much more effectively."

As Paul Tournier pointed out: "It is only when a husband and wife pray together before God that they find the secret of true

---

7. When you are in the wrong, admit it and ask for forgiveness. (James 5:16) When someone confesses to you, tell them you forgive them. Be sure their failure is *forgotten* and not brought up by you again. (Proverbs 17:9; Ephesians 4:32; Colossians 3:13; 1 Peter 4:8)
8. Avoid nagging. (Proverbs 10:19; 17:9; 20:5)
9. Do not blame or criticize the other person. Instead, restore, encourage, edify. (Proverbs 25:11; Romans 14:13; Galatians 6:1; 1 Thessalonians 5:11) If someone verbally attacks, criticizes, or blames you, do not respond in the same manner. (Romans 12:17, 21; 1 Peter 2:23; 3:9)
10. Try to understand the other person's opinion. Make allowances for differences. Be concerned about their interests. (Philippians 2:1-4; Ephesians 4:2)

Our Agreement to Follow These Guidelines

Name_____

Name_____

Date_____

harmony, that the difference in their temperaments, their ideas, and their tastes enriches their home instead of endangering it. There will be no further question of one imposing his will on the other or of the other giving in for the sake of peace. Instead, they will together seek God's will, which alone will ensure that each will be fully able to develop his personality. . . .

"When each of the marriage partners seeks quietly before God to see his own faults, recognizes his sin, and asks the forgiveness of the other, marital problems are no more. Each learns to speak the other's language, and to meet him halfway, so to speak. Each holds back those harsh little words which one is apt to utter when one is right, but which are said in order to injure. Most of all, a couple rediscovers complete mutual confidence because in meditating in prayer together they learn to become absolutely honest with each other. . . . This is the price to be paid if partners very different from each other are to combine their gifts instead of setting them against each other."[6]

In fact, many of the ideas in this book, especially those that suggest or imply changes either spouse must make, will be impossible to achieve or use without prayer. God is the one who can change a marriage—not manuals or books!

Notes

INTRODUCTION
1. Charles Shedd, *Letters to Phillip* (Old Tappan, N.J.: Spire Books, 1969), 82-83.

CHAPTER 1
1. Reuel Howe, *Herein Is Love* (Valley Forge, Penn.: Judson Press, 1961), 100.
2. Adapted from Dwight H. Small *After You've Said I Do* (Old Tappan, N.J.: Fleming H. Revell, 1968), 106-107, 112.
3. Adapted from Cecil Osborne *The Art of Understanding Yourself* (Grand Rapids, Mich.: Zondervan, 1967), chapter 9.

CHAPTER 2
1. Adapted from John Powell, *Why Am I Afraid to Tell You Who I Am?* (Allen, Tex.: Argus Communications, 1982), 54-62.

CHAPTER 3
1. William C. Menninger, "Behind Many Flaws of Society," *National Observer* 31 August 1964, 18.
2. David Augsburger, *Be All You Can Be* (Altamonte Springs, Fla.: Creation House), 60.
3. Powell, *Why Am I Afraid to Tell You Who I Am?* 155.
4. Augsburger, *Be All You Can Be,* 31-32.

CHAPTER 4

1. James A. Hadfield, *Psychology and Morals* (New York: Barnes and Noble, 1964), 35.
2. Adapted from Powell, *Why Am I Afraid to Tell You Who I Am?* 91-92.
3. Robert McFarland and John Burton, *Learning for Loving* (Grand Rapids, Mich.: Zondervan, 1969), 93.
4. Small, *After You've Said I Do,* 75.
5. Virginia Satir, *Conjoint Family Therapy* (Palo Alto, Calif.: Science and Behavior Books, Inc., 1967), 73.
6. Howard J. Clinebell, *The Intimate Marriage* (New York: Harper & Row, 1970), 99.
7. Small, *After You've Said I Do,* 137, 154.

CHAPTER 5

1. Adapted from Albert Ellis and Robert Harper, *Creative Marriage* (Secaucus, N.J.: Lyle Stuart, 1961), 190-191.
2. Clinebell, *The Intimate Marriage,* 93.
3. John Edmund Haggai, *How to Win over Worry* (Grand Rapids, Mich.: Zondervan, 1959), 63-64.

CHAPTER 6

1. Dorothy Briggs, *Your Child's Self-Esteem: The Key to His Life* (New York: Doubleday), 3.
2. Paul Tournier, *To Understand Each Other* (Atlanta, Ga.: John Knox Press, 1962), 58.
3. Fritz Ridenour, *How to Be a Christian without Being Religious* (Ventura, Calif.: Regal Books, 1967), 147-148.
4. Ibid., 126.
5. Paul Tournier, *The Healing of Persons* (New York: Harper & Row, 1965), 88-89.

About the Author

H. NORMAN WRIGHT is founder and director of Christian Marriage Enrichment and Family Counseling and Enrichment in Santa Ana, California. He is a licensed marriage, family, and child counselor and has authored more than fifty books. Norm has taught at Biola University and is currently on the faculty of Talbot Theological Seminary.

Bible Broadcasting Network
Post Office Box 1818
Chesapeake, Virginia 23320
(804) 547-9421   1-800-888-7077

ALABAMA
Birmingham 98.5
Decatur 91.7
Dothan 89.5
Huntsville 106.3

BERMUDA
VSB 1280

FLORIDA
Englewood 91.3
Gainesville 90.5
Lakeland 91.9
Tarpon Springs 88.9

GEORGIA
Atlanta 1420 (AM)
Augusta 100.9
Columbus 89.5
Savannah 89.5
Swainsboro 88.7

KANSAS
Wichita 88.3

NEW YORK
Schroon Lake 91.1

NORTH CAROLINA
Aberdeen 89.9
Charlotte 930 (AM)
Fayetteville 106.3
Henderson 92.5
High Point 95.5
Pinehurst 89.9
Southern Pines 89.9
Whispering Pines 89.9

OHIO
Belpre 89.5

Clyde 90.5
Lancaster 90.9

SOUTH CAROLINA
Columbia 88.7
Gaffney 91.1
N. Charleston 90.7

TENNESSEE
Chattanooga 89.7
Knoxville 95.3
Nashville 980 (AM)

VIRGINIA
Ashland 100.1
Blacksburg 100.1
Bassett 107.1
Charlottesville 95.9
Christiansburg 100.1
Danville 92.7
Fairlawn 100.1
Fredericksburg 92.1
Harrisonburg 107.1
Luray 103.9
Martinsville 107.1
Norfolk 99.7
Pulaski 97.7
Radford 100.1
Roanoke 97.7
Salem 97.7
Stafford 92.1
Westover Hills 92.7
Wytheville 92.7

WEST VIRGINIA
Parkersburg 89.5
Princeton 91.1